The Catholi Prayer Book

Belongs to: ______________________________

Given by: ______________________________

Date: ______________________________

My Faith Journey

Date of Baptism: ______________________________

Date of First Reconciliation: ______________________________

Date of First Eucharist: ______________________________

Contents

Everyday Prayers

Rosary Prayers

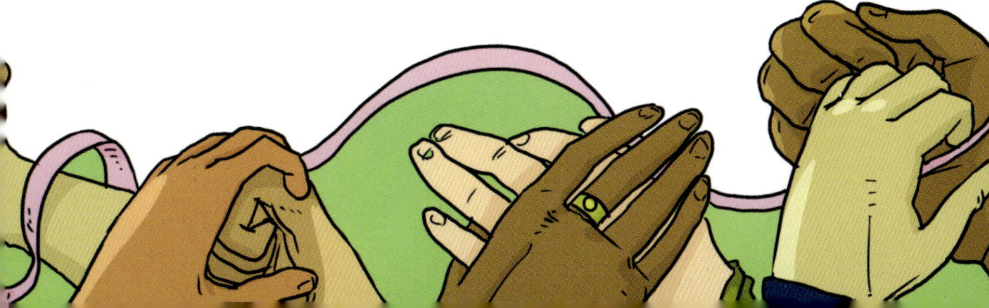

Prayers for the Church Seasons

Bible Passages for Special Times

Everyday Practices

The Celebration of Reconciliation

Introduction

There is an old church song that begins with the line "What a friend we have in Jesus," and it is true. God loves each one of us and wants nothing more than to be our lifelong friend.

Prayer is our way of talking to God. In prayer, we tell God what we need, we tell God we love him, and we ask God to be with us in everything we do. Sometimes we talk to God quietly in our hearts, and we know that God hears us. Other times, we talk to God using words other people have written. Those people know and love God and want us to know and love him as well.

In this book, you will find prayers to deepen your friendship with God. These prayers will help you talk to God and help you find ways during the day to stop, just for a minute, and offer a prayer. The prayers in this book will also help you talk to God as part of the Church, as you pray the prayers of the Mass and the Rosary.

Praying every day helps you realize how much God loves you, and it also helps you love God. As you come to know God more and more through prayer, you will grow in your love for him. We hope these prayers help you do that.

The Order and Prayers of the Mass

I. Introductory Rites

In the Introductory Rites, we gather and prepare ourselves to celebrate the Eucharist.

1. Entrance Chant

We stand and sing a hymn. The priest, along with others who will serve at the Mass, process to the altar.

2. Greeting

We make the Sign of the Cross. The priest welcomes us and prays that God will give us blessings in the Mass. The priest can use several greetings.

Priest: In the name of the Father, and of the Son, and of the Holy Spirit.

People: Amen.

Priest: The grace of our Lord Jesus Christ, and the love of God, and the communion of the Holy Spirit be with you all.

People: And with your spirit.

3. Penitential Act

Using one of the forms of the Penitential Act, we pray to God to have mercy on us.

Penitential Act, Form A

I confess to almighty God
and to you, my brothers and sisters,
that I have greatly sinned,
in my thoughts and in my words,
in what I have done and in what I have failed to do,
(We strike our breast as we say the following two lines.)
through my fault, through my fault,
through my most grievous fault;
therefore I ask blessed Mary ever-Virgin,
all the Angels and Saints,
and you, my brothers and sisters,
to pray for me to the Lord our God.

Penitential Act, Form B

Priest: Have mercy on us, O Lord.

People: For we have sinned against you.

Priest: Show us, O Lord, your mercy.

People: And grant us your salvation.

Lord Have Mercy

Priest: Lord, have mercy.

People: Lord, have mercy.

Priest: Christ, have mercy.

People: Christ, have mercy.

Priest: Lord, have mercy.

People: Lord, have mercy.

Priest: May almighty God have mercy on us, forgive us our sins, and bring us to everlasting life.

People: Amen.

4. Gloria

On most Sundays, we praise God by praying or singing the **Gloria**.

Gloria

Glory to God in the highest,
and on earth peace to people of good will.

We praise you,
we bless you,
we adore you,
we glorify you,
we give you thanks for your great glory,
Lord God, heavenly King,
O God, almighty Father.

Lord Jesus Christ, Only Begotten Son,
Lord God, Lamb of God, Son of the Father,
you take away the sins of the world,
have mercy on us;
you take away the sins of the world,
receive our prayer;
you are seated at the right hand
of the Father,
have mercy on us.

For you alone are the Holy One,
you alone are the Lord,
you alone are the Most High,
Jesus Christ,
with the Holy Spirit,
in the glory of God the Father.
Amen.

5. Collect (Opening Prayer)

The priest invites us to pray. We pause for a moment of silent prayer that helps us remember that we are in the presence of God. Then the priest says a prayer and we respond.

Priest: Let us pray. . . .

People: Amen.

II. Liturgy of the Word

The Liturgy of the Word is the part of the Mass when we hear God's Word proclaimed. Hearing and reflecting on God's Word helps make us ready to receive the Body and Blood of Christ during the Liturgy of the Eucharist.

1. First Reading

We listen closely to a reading from the Old Testament or the Acts of the Apostles. At the end of the reading, we say:

Reader: The word of the Lord.

People: Thanks be to God.

2. Responsorial Psalm

The cantor or reader sings or says the verses of a psalm from the Old Testament, and we give the response.

3. Second Reading

Again we listen closely to a Scripture reading. This reading is from the letters in the New Testament or the Acts of the Apostles. At the end of the reading, we say:

Reader: The word of the Lord.

People: Thanks be to God.

4. Alleluia or Gospel Acclamation

We stand for the Gospel Acclamation. On most Sundays, we sing, "Alleluia!," which means "Praise the Lord."

5. Gospel Reading

We listen closely to a reading from the Gospels proclaimed by the priest or deacon. Before we hear the Gospel reading, we say:

Priest or deacon: The Lord be with you.

People: And with your spirit.

Priest or deacon: A reading from the holy Gospel according to . . .

People: Glory to you, O Lord.

We all make the Sign of the Cross on our foreheads, lips, and heart.

After the reading, we respond:

Priest or deacon: The Gospel of the Lord.

People: Praise to you, Lord Jesus Christ.

6. Homily

The priest or deacon talks to us about the Scriptures and their meaning for our lives.

7. Profession of Faith

We stand and profess our faith by praying either the **Nicene Creed** or the **Apostles' Creed**.

Nicene Creed

I believe in one God,
the Father almighty,
maker of heaven and earth,
of all things visible and invisible.

I believe in one Lord Jesus Christ,
the Only Begotten Son of God,
born of the Father before all ages.
God from God, Light from Light,
true God from true God,
begotten, not made, consubstantial with the Father;
through him all things were made.
For us men and for our salvation
he came down from heaven,
(We bow as we say the following two lines.)
and by the Holy Spirit was incarnate of the Virgin Mary,
and became man.

For our sake he was crucified under Pontius Pilate,
he suffered death and was buried,
and rose again on the third day
in accordance with the Scriptures.
He ascended into heaven
and is seated at the right hand of the Father.
He will come again in glory
to judge the living and the dead
and his kingdom will have no end.

I believe in the Holy Spirit, the Lord, the giver of life,
who proceeds from the Father and the Son,
who with the Father and the Son is adored and glorified,
who has spoken through the prophets.

I believe in one, holy, catholic, and apostolic Church.
I confess one Baptism for the forgiveness of sins
and I look forward to the resurrection of the dead
and the life of the world to come. Amen.

Apostles' Creed

I believe in God,
the Father almighty,
Creator of heaven and earth,
and in Jesus Christ, his only Son, our Lord,
(We bow as we say the following two lines.)
who was conceived by the Holy Spirit,
born of the Virgin Mary,
suffered under Pontius Pilate,
was crucified, died and was buried;
he descended into hell;

on the third day he rose again from the dead;
he ascended into heaven,
and is seated at the right hand of God the Father almighty;
from there he will come to judge the living and the dead.

I believe in the Holy Spirit,
the holy catholic Church,
the communion of saints,
the forgiveness of sins,
the resurrection of the body,
and life everlasting.

Amen.

8. Universal Prayer (Prayer of the Faithful)

We pray for the needs of the Church and people everywhere.

III. Liturgy of the Eucharist

The Liturgy of the Eucharist is the core of the Mass. The gifts of bread and wine are brought to the altar and we give thanks to God. The gifts of bread and wine become the Body and Blood of Christ, and those who are prepared to do so receive Holy Communion.

1. Presentation and Preparation of the Gifts

Altar servers prepare the altar for the gifts, and members of the assembly bring the gifts of bread and wine to the altar. We usually sing during this preparation.

The priest holds the bread above the altar and prays:

Priest: Blessed are you, Lord God of all creation,
for through your goodness we have received
the bread we offer you:
fruit of the earth and work of human hands,
it will become for us the bread of life.

People: Blessed be God for ever.

The priest holds the chalice filled with wine above the altar and prays:

Priest: Blessed are you, Lord God of all creation,
for through your goodness we have received
the wine we offer you:
fruit of the vine and work of human hands,
it will become our spiritual drink.

People: Blessed be God for ever.

The priest then prays, and we ask God to accept our gifts:

Priest: Pray, brethren (brothers and sisters), that my sacrifice and yours may be acceptable to God, the almighty Father.

People: May the Lord accept the sacrifice at your hands for the praise and glory of his name, for our good and the good of all his holy Church.

2. Prayer over the Offerings

The priest prays over the gifts of bread and wine, and we respond "Amen."

3. Eucharistic Prayer

This is the Church's great prayer of thanksgiving. The priest leads the prayer, and the assembly prays the responses.

Preface Dialogue

We give thanks to God by singing or saying:

Priest: The Lord be with you.

People: And with your spirit.

Priest: Lift up your hearts.

People: We lift them up to the Lord.

Priest: Let us give thanks to the Lord our God.

People: It is right and just.

Then the priest sings or says the Preface of the Eucharistic Prayer.

Acclamation (Holy, Holy, Holy)

With the priest we sing or say:

Holy, Holy, Holy

Holy, Holy, Holy Lord God of hosts.
Heaven and earth are full of your glory.
Hosanna in the highest.
Blessed is he who comes in the name of the Lord.
Hosanna in the highest.

The priest then praises God, and prays for the needs of the Church. Then he recalls what Jesus did and said at the Last Supper.

Consecration

Taking the bread, the priest prays:

Priest: Take this, all of you, and eat of it,
for this is my Body,
which will be given up for you.

The priest holds up the consecrated bread, or Host, which, through the priest's words and actions and the power of the Holy Spirit, is now the Body of Christ.

The priest takes the wine and says the words of Jesus:

Priest: Take this, all of you, and drink from it,
for this is the chalice of my Blood,
the Blood of the new and eternal covenant,
which will be poured out for you and for many
for the forgiveness of sins.

Do this in memory of me.

The priest holds up the consecrated wine, which through the priest's words and actions and the power of the Holy Spirit, is now the Blood of Christ.

Memorial Acclamation

Priest: The mystery of faith.

People: When we eat this Bread and drink this Cup, we proclaim your Death, O Lord, until you come again.

or

People: We proclaim your Death, O Lord, and profess your Resurrection until you come again.

or

People: Save us, Savior of the world, for by your Cross and Resurrection you have set us free.

The priest asks God the Father to remember the Church throughout the world and to help us all grow in love and unity. He finishes by holding up the Body and Blood of Christ and singing or praying:

Priest: Through him, and with him, and in him, O God, almighty Father, in the unity of the Holy Spirit, all glory and honor is yours, for ever and ever.

People: Amen.

4. Communion Rite

The Communion Rite is the name for the part of the Liturgy of the Eucharist that begins with the Lord's Prayer. During the Communion Rite, those who are prepared can receive Holy Communion, the Body and Blood of Christ. The word *communion* means "unity" or "oneness."

Lord's Prayer (Our Father)

We pray to God the Father with the prayer that Jesus taught us.

Lord's Prayer

Our Father, who art in heaven,
hallowed be thy name;
thy kingdom come,
thy will be done
on earth as it is in heaven.
Give us this day our daily bread,
and forgive us our trespasses,
as we forgive those who trespass against us;
and lead us not into temptation,
but deliver us from evil.

After the priest prays a prayer to grant us peace and freedom from distress, we pray:

For the kingdom,
the power and the glory are yours
now and for ever.

Sign of Peace

We are invited to share a Sign of Peace with one another.

Priest: The peace of the Lord be with you always.

People: And with your spirit.

Priest: Let us offer each other the sign of peace.

Breaking of the Bread (Lamb of God)

The priest breaks the Host. During this, we sing or say:

Lamb of God

Lamb of God, you take away the sins of the world,
have mercy on us.
Lamb of God, you take away the sins of the world,
have mercy on us.
Lamb of God, you take away the sins of the world,
grant us peace.

Invitation to Communion

The priest holds up the Body of Christ and invites us to receive Holy Communion.

Priest: Behold the Lamb of God,
behold him who takes away the sins of the world.
Blessed are those called to the supper of the Lamb.

People: Lord, I am not worthy
that you should enter under my roof,
but only say the word
and my soul shall be healed.

Communion

The priest receives Holy Communion. We then receive Holy Communion:

Priest: The Body of Christ.

People: Amen.

We may also be invited to receive the Blood of Christ:

Priest: The Blood of Christ.

People: Amen.

We return to our seats and pray quietly, giving thanks for the gift of the Eucharist.

Prayer after Communion

The priest prays a prayer after everyone has received Holy Communion. We respond "Amen."

IV. Concluding Rites

We are blessed and dismissed by the priest.

1. Greeting

The priest invites us to pray.

Priest: The Lord be with you.

People: And with your spirit.

2. Final Blessing

The priest offers us a final blessing.

Priest: May Almighty God bless you, the Father, and the Son, and the Holy Spirit.

People: Amen.

3. Dismissal

The priest or deacon dismisses us, inviting us to serve God in these or similar words:

Priest or deacon: Go forth, the Mass is ended.

People: Thanks be to God.

We sing a closing hymn, and the priest and other ministers process out.

Everyday Prayers

Sign of the Cross

In the name of the Father,
and of the Son,
and of the Holy Spirit. Amen.

How to Make the Sign of the Cross

Grace before Meals

Bless us, O Lord, and these your gifts,
which we are about to receive
from your bounty,
through Christ our Lord. Amen.

Grace after Meals

We give you thanks, almighty God,
for these and all your gifts,
which we have received
through Christ our Lord. Amen.

Morning Prayer

O my God, I offer you this day,
all I do and think and say.
In union with what was done
on earth by Jesus Christ,
your Son.
Amen.

Evening Prayer

God, our Father, this day is done.
We ask you and Jesus Christ, your Son,
that with the Spirit, our welcome guest,
you guard our sleep and bless our rest.
Amen.

Act of Faith

O my God, I firmly believe that you are one God in three Divine Persons, Father, Son, and Holy Spirit. I believe that your divine Son became man and died for our sins and that he will come to judge the living and the dead. I believe these and all the truths which the Holy Catholic Church teaches because you have revealed them who are eternal truth and wisdom, who can neither deceive nor be deceived. In this faith I intend to live and die. Amen.

Act of Hope

O Lord God, I hope by your grace for the pardon of all my sins, and after life here to gain eternal happiness because you have promised it, who are infinitely powerful, faithful, kind, and merciful. In this hope I intend to live and die. Amen.

Act of Love

O Lord God, I love you above all things and I love my neighbor for your sake because you are the highest, infinite, and perfect good, worthy of all my love. In this love I intend to live and die. Amen.

A Prayer to Jesus
(by Saint Richard of Chichester)

O most merciful Redeemer, Friend,
and Brother,
May I know you more clearly,
Love you more dearly,
And follow you more nearly,
For ever and ever. Amen.

Angel of God

Angel of God, my guardian dear,
to whom God's love commits me here,
ever this day be at my side,
to light and guard, to rule and guide. Amen.

Prayer of Saint Francis of Assisi

(Peace Prayer of Saint Francis)

Lord, make me an instrument of your peace.
Where there is hatred, let me sow love;
where there is injury, pardon;
where there is doubt, faith;
where there is despair, hope;
where there is darkness, light;
where there is sadness, joy.
O Divine Master, grant that I may not so much
seek to be consoled as to console;
to be understood as to understand;
to be loved as to love.
For it is in giving that we receive;
it is in pardoning that we are pardoned;
and it is in dying that we are born to eternal life.
Amen.

Rosary Prayers

Mysteries of the Rosary

There are twenty mysteries of the life of Jesus that we meditate on when praying the Rosary.

Joyful Mysteries

1. The Annunciation
2. The Visitation
3. The Birth of Our Lord
4. The Presentation of Jesus in the Temple
5. The Finding of Jesus in the Temple

Luminous Mysteries

1. The Baptism of Jesus
2. Jesus Reveals Himself in the Miracle at Cana
3. Jesus Proclaims the Good News of the Kingdom of God
4. The Transfiguration of Jesus
5. The Institution of the Eucharist

Sorrowful Mysteries

1. The Agony of Jesus in the Garden
2. The Scourging at the Pillar
3. The Crowning with Thorns
4. The Carrying of the Cross
5. The Crucifixion

Glorious Mysteries

1. The Resurrection of Jesus
2. The Ascension of Jesus into Heaven
3. The Descent of the Holy Spirit upon the Apostles
4. The Assumption of Mary into Heaven
5. The Crowning of Mary as Queen of Heaven

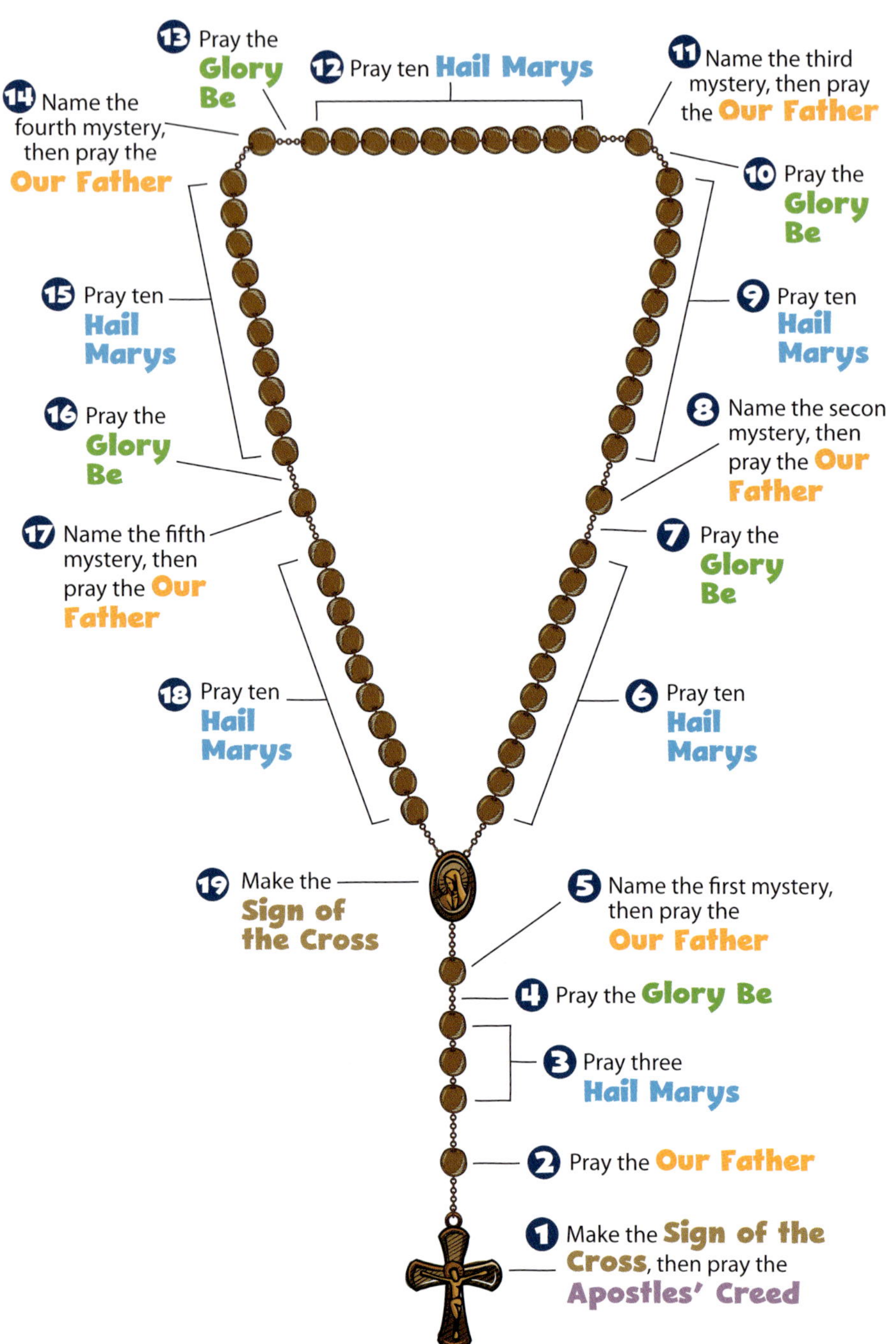
1 Make the Sign of the Cross, then pray the Apostles' Creed
2 Pray the Our Father
3 Pray three Hail Marys
4 Pray the Glory Be
5 Name the first mystery, then pray the Our Father
6 Pray ten Hail Marys
7 Pray the Glory Be
8 Name the second mystery, then pray the Our Father
9 Pray ten Hail Marys
10 Pray the Glory Be
11 Name the third mystery, then pray the Our Father
12 Pray ten Hail Marys
13 Pray the Glory Be
14 Name the fourth mystery, then pray the Our Father
15 Pray ten Hail Marys
16 Pray the Glory Be
17 Name the fifth mystery, then pray the Our Father
18 Pray ten Hail Marys
19 Make the Sign of the Cross

Sign of the Cross

In the name of the Father,
and of the Son,
and of the Holy Spirit. Amen.

Apostles' Creed

I believe in God,
the Father almighty,
Creator of heaven and earth,
and in Jesus Christ, his only Son, our Lord,
who was conceived by the Holy Spirit,
born of the Virgin Mary,
suffered under Pontius Pilate,
was crucified, died and was buried;
he descended into hell;
on the third day he rose again from the dead;
he ascended into heaven,
and is seated at the right hand of God the
Father almighty;
from there he will come to judge the living
and the dead.

I believe in the Holy Spirit,
the holy catholic Church,
the communion of saints,
the forgiveness of sins,
the resurrection of the body,
and life everlasting.
Amen.

Our Father (Lord's Prayer)

Our Father, who art in heaven,
hallowed be thy name.
Thy kingdom come;
thy will be done
on earth as it is in heaven.
Give us this day our daily bread;
and forgive us our trespasses
as we forgive those
who trespass against us;
and lead us not into temptation,
but deliver us from evil. Amen.

Hail Mary

Hail Mary, full of grace,
the Lord is with thee.
Blessed art thou among women,
and blessed is the fruit of thy
womb, Jesus.
Holy Mary, Mother of God,
pray for us sinners,
now and at the hour of our death.
Amen.

Glory Be

Glory be to the Father,
and to the Son,
and to the Holy Spirit.
As it was in the beginning,
is now,
and will be forever. Amen.

Hail, Holy Queen

(This is prayed at the end of the Rosary.)

Hail, Holy Queen, Mother of mercy,
our life, our sweetness and our hope.
To you do we cry, poor banished
children of Eve.
To you do we send up our sighs,
mourning and weeping in this valley of tears.
Turn then, most gracious advocate,
your eyes of mercy toward us,
and after this exile show to us the blessed
fruit of your womb, Jesus.
O clement, O loving,
O sweet Virgin Mary.

Fatima Prayer

(Some people include this prayer after the Glory Be at the end of each set of ten Hail Marys.)

O my Jesus,
forgive us our sins,
save us from the fires of hell,
lead all souls to heaven,
especially those in most need of your mercy.
Amen.

Prayers for the Church Seasons

Lord Jesus, you are Emmanuel, God with us. Thank for you coming to live among us. Help us to prepare to celebrate your birth at Christmas with peaceful and loving hearts. We ask this in your name, Lord Jesus. Amen.

Lord Jesus, fill our hearts with joy as we prepare and wait for you to come at Christmas. And so we pray: Come, Lord Jesus! Amen.

God, our Father, we ask you to be with us as we prepare for the coming of your Son, Jesus. Show us how to make room in our lives for his love and peace. Amen.

O God, bless our homes, our families, and our friends as we prepare for Christmas. Teach us to wait in joyful hope and to be kind to one another. We ask this in the name of Jesus. Amen.

Loving God, you sent your Son, Jesus, to show us the way to you. Help us to follow your way every day and to grow closer to you this Advent season. We ask this through Christ, our Lord. Amen.

Jesus, you came to bring your life and love to all people. You fill our hearts with your grace. Help us to share your gifts with all the people we meet. Amen.

Loving God, you sent your Good News of Jesus' birth through the message of an angel. Open our ears, our eyes, and our hearts so we can receive all the messages of love that you send to us. Amen.

Dear God, guide me to a closer relationship with Jesus and help me to offer gifts of joy to others during this Christmas season and throughout the year. Amen.

Thank you, God, for the gift of your Son, Jesus, who came to live as one of us. Help us to live in his light and to walk in his way. Amen.

Lord Jesus, speak to us your word of love and faithfulness. Help us to share your love with others and to celebrate with joy and peace your coming among us as a human being at Christmas. We ask this in your name. Amen.

(Palm Sunday)
Lord, God, may this Palm Sunday help us to praise you always. Thank you for the gift of new life in your Son, Jesus, our King. Hosanna in the highest! Amen.

God, you are a loving father who forgives his children. Help us to be kind. Help us to love. Help us to forgive. We ask this in the name of Jesus Christ, our Lord. Amen.

Loving God, you walk with us through all moments of life. You take us through every challenge and every struggle. Fill our life with your Spirit, give us courage to make good choices, and bring us closer to you. Amen.

Dear God, we remember that our Baptism made us members of your family, the Church. Help us to understand the meaning of the season of Lent and how we might use this time to come closer to you. Amen.

Jesus, you suffered and died for us. Help us to understand your great love that would offer yourself to free us from sin and death. Show us the path of love that you walked. Amen.

Jesus, you bring us new life, now and always. May we celebrate the Easter season with joy and love. Amen.

God of all, help us to share the Good News of your love with those around us. Help us to follow Jesus and let others see us as a people of hope and new life. Amen.

Jesus, because of you, we have hope for new life. You brought hope to your friends, and you continue to bring hope to all people. Fill our hearts with your hope. We ask this in your name. Amen.

Jesus, help us to follow you when we don't understand. Open our hearts to recognize you. Be with us as learn more about your presence with us. Amen.

Risen Lord Jesus, we rejoice at your Resurrection! We say, "Christ is risen. Alleluia! Let us bless the Lord! Alleluia! Thanks be to God! Alleluia! Alleluia! Alleluia!"

Loving God, you sent your Son, Jesus, to Earth to save us, and the Holy Spirit to guide us. Help us welcome the Holy Spirit into our hearts. We ask this in the name of the Father and of the Son and of the Holy Spirit. Amen.

Come, Holy Spirit. Fill us with hope and love. Guide us and help us to follow Jesus always. Amen.

Come, Holy Spirit, and fill us with courage and enthusiasm so that we may spread the message of Jesus in word and action to all those we meet. Amen.

Come Holy Spirit, fill our hearts with your love. Inspire us, renew the earth, and bring us joy. Amen.

Heavenly Father, you sent your Son, Jesus, to Earth to save us, and you sent the Holy Spirit to change our lives forever. Open our hearts and fill us with your Spirit. Please work through us to spread your Good News. Amen.

Dear Jesus, you teach us how to live. Open our hearts to hear your teachings and to follow them. We ask this in your name. Amen.

Lord, we learn many things about your great love for us throughout the year. Help us to spread that love to others through our words and our actions. Amen.

Loving God, you want us to come closer to you every day. Help us learn how to listen for your answer. We ask this in the name of Jesus, your Son. Amen.

Lord Jesus, help us to live our ordinary lives in an extraordinary way, by following your teachings in faith, hope, and love. Amen.

Dear Jesus, we thank you for the love you show us. Help us to welcome others in the same way you welcomed and treated all people. Teach us your ways and let us be a sign of your love and hope in our world. Amen.

Prayers with My Family

God, thank you for the gifts you have given to each of us. Help us as a family to share our gifts with others so that they may know your love for them. Amen.

God our Father, help us as a family to love you more. May our hearts be filled with thanks for all that you do for us. Amen.

Thank you, God, for *(invite each member of the family to share one thing)*. We praise you, God. Let our family life be a song of praise to you! Amen.

God, we ask for your strength to love you and others the way we should. Help our family to make every moment in our lives an example of your love. We ask this in Jesus' name. Amen.

Thank you, God, for being so kind and loving to us. Help our family to look for ways throughout our day to share that same kindness with others. We ask this in your name. Amen.

God, we ask for help to not worry about the things in our life. Thank you for taking care of our family in every little part of our day. We will trust in you with our whole hearts. Amen.

Jesus, open our eyes so we can see you! Fill the hearts in our family with joy and praise, for you are always with us, loving us and helping us each day. In your name, we pray. Amen.

Dear Jesus, you taught us that we must love one another. Help our family to show love to others in our words and actions, especially to those who are poor and in need. Amen.

God our Father, you blessed us with all living creatures. Help our family to share in your love for all creatures by taking care of, protecting, and treating them well. Amen.

Loving God, the saints show us that holiness is possible for all of us. Help our family use the example of the saints to become more loving in our own lives. We ask this through Christ our Lord. Amen.

Dear God, thank you for the blessing of our family. Help us to be more forgiving of one another in our everyday struggles. Help us to be kind and loving to one another every day. Amen.

Gracious God, we thank you for our family. Help us to remember that in Baptism, we become part of a bigger family, your Church. Bless our family, the Church, and the work that we do to serve you together. Amen.

Bible Passages for Special Times

When I am feeling happy:

- Psalm 117
- Psalm 150
- Philippians 4:4–7

When I am feeling sad:

- Psalm 36:5–10
- Romans 8:38–39
- Revelation 21:1–4

When I am feeling afraid:

- Psalm 27
- Luke 12:22–31
- John 14:27

When I want to say thank you to God:

- 1 Chronicles 16:28–34
- Psalm 30
- 1 Thessalonians 5:16–18

When I have hurt someone:

- Psalm 51
- Mark 11:24–25
- 1 John 2:9–12

When someone has hurt me:

- Psalm 6
- Matthew 18:21–22
- Luke 6:27–31

When I need a reminder of God's love:

- Jeremiah 31:3 or Psalm 117
- John 13:1
- 1 John 3:1

When someone I know needs God's help:

- Psalm 5:1–3
- Matthew 7:7–11
- James 5:13–16

When things aren't going my way:

- Psalm 31:24
- Jeremiah 29:11–13
- Romans 15:13

When I am worried:

- Proverbs 12:25
- Matthew 11:28–30
- Philippians 4:6–7

When I need to be strong:

- Psalm 18:28–32
- Psalm 23
- Ephesians 3:16–18

When I begin something new:

- Psalm 90:17
- Psalm 98:1
- Revelation 21:5

When I must wait on God:

- Psalm 130:5–7
- Proverbs 15:18
- James 5:7–8

When I pray for peace:

- John 14:27
- Philippians 4:6–7
- 2 Thessalonians 3:16

When I give thanks for a friend:

- Proverbs 18:24
- Sirach 6:14–17
- John 15:12–15

When I pray for my family:

- Acts 16:31
- Romans 15:5–6
- Ephesians 6:1–4

Everyday Practices

Golden Rule

"Do for others what you want them to do for you." (Matthew 7:12)

Ten Commandments

1. I am the Lord your God, you shall not have other gods before me.
2. You shall not take the name of the Lord your God in vain.
3. Remember to keep holy the Lord's Day.
4. Honor your father and your mother.
5. You shall not kill.
6. You shall not commit adultery.
7. You shall not steal.
8. You shall not bear false witness against your neighbor.
9. You shall not covet your neighbor's wife.
10. You shall not covet your neighbor's possessions.

(Based on Exodus 20:1–17. For more on the Ten Commandments, see Exodus, chapter 20, in *The Catholic Children's Bible.*)

Beatitudes

Blessed are the poor in spirit,
for theirs is the Kingdom of heaven.
Blessed are they who mourn,
for they will be comforted.
Blessed are the meek,
for they will inherit the land.
Blessed are they who hunger and thirst
for righteousness,for they will be satisfied.
Blessed are the merciful,
for they will be shown mercy.
Blessed are the clean of heart,
for they will see God.
Blessed are the peacemakers,
for they will be called children of God.
Blessed are they who are persecuted for the sake of
righteousness, for theirs is the kingdom of heaven.

(Based on Matthew 5:3–10. For more on the Beatitudes, see Matthew, chapters 5–7, and Luke, chapter 6, in *The Catholic Children's Bible*.)

Corporal Works of Mercy

1. Feed the hungry.
2. Give drink to the thirsty.
3. Clothe the naked.
4. Shelter the homeless.
5. Visit the sick.
6. Visit the imprisoned.
7. Bury the dead.

Spiritual Works of Mercy

1. Counsel the doubtful.
2. Teach the ignorant.
3. Help the sinner.
4. Comfort the afflicted.
5. Forgive injuries.
6. Bear wrongs patiently.
7. Pray for the living and the dead.

Seven Sacraments

1. Baptism
2. Confirmation
3. Holy Eucharist
4. Penance and Reconciliation
5. Anointing of the Sick
6. Holy Orders
7. Matrimony

Holy Days of Obligation

Solemnity of Mary, Mother of God (January 1)
Ascension (40 days from Easter Sunday; may be celebrated on the last Thursday or Sunday before Pentecost)
Assumption of Mary (August 15)
All Saints' Day (November 1)
Immaculate Conception (December 8)
Christmas (December 25)

Precepts of the Church

1. Participate in Mass on Sundays and holy days of obligation. Keep these days holy. Avoid unnecessary work.
2. Confess your sins in the Sacrament of Penance and Reconciliation at least once each year.
3. Receive Holy Communion at least once a year, during the Easter season.
4. Follow the rules of fasting and abstaining from meat on the special days of Ash Wednesday, Good Friday, and the Fridays of Lent.
5. Give what you can to help meet the needs of the Church.

Stations of the Cross

1. Jesus is condemned to death.
2. Jesus takes up his cross.
3. Jesus falls the first time.
4. Jesus meets his mother.
5. Simon helps Jesus carry the cross.
6. Veronica wipes the face of Jesus.
7. Jesus falls the second time.
8. Jesus meets the women of Jerusalem.
9. Jesus falls the third time.
10. Jesus is stripped of his garments.
11. Jesus is nailed to the cross.
12. Jesus dies on the cross.
13. Jesus is taken down from the cross.
14. Jesus is laid in the tomb.

The Celebration of Reconciliation

Communal Celebration

1. We gather with our parish community. We join in singing a hymn. The priest greets us and leads us in praying together.
2. We listen to the Bible. We may hear more than one reading, with a psalm response in between. We stand for the Gospel reading. Then we listen to the priest or deacon talk about the readings. He helps us understand what we heard in Scripture.
3. We make an examination of conscience. We think of things we have done that we are sorry for. We pray together to tell God we are sorry. Then we pray the Lord's Prayer together.
4. We wait to take our turn confessing our sins. While we wait, we can sing or pray. When it is my turn, I confess my sins. The priest gives me my penance and absolves me from my sins. My sins are forgiven! I make the Sign of the Cross with the priest.
5. When everyone has confessed individually, we pray and sing in thanksgiving to God. The priest or deacon blesses us. We go in peace.
6. I do my penance as soon as possible.

Individual Celebration

1. I take time to examine my conscience. I ask the Holy Spirit to help me remember what I have done or not done to follow God's Law. I think about the words of Jesus ("Love one another"), the Ten Commandments, and the Golden Rule.
2. The priest welcomes me. We make the Sign of the Cross together.
3. We read from the Bible. The priest may ask me to read.
4. I confess my sins to the priest. He may give me some words of advice or encouragement. Then he gives me my penance.
5. The priest invites me to pray an Act of Contrition. In my prayer, I tell God that I am sorry for what I have done wrong and that I will try not to do these things again.
6. The priest extends his hand or hands over me and gives me absolution in the name of Jesus. My sins are forgiven! I make the Sign of the Cross with the priest.
7. We give thanks to God, and then the priest sends me forth in peace. I do my penance as soon as possible. I quietly thank Jesus for giving me his new life of grace and a new start.

Receive the Sacrament of Reconciliation often. It will help you to follow Jesus. The Church wants us to receive this sacrament at least once a year. Those who have committed a mortal sin must confess their sins and receive absolution before receiving Holy Communion.

Examination of Conscience

Think about the words of Jesus: "Love one another as I have loved you." Ask the Holy Spirit to bring to your mind what you have done, or what you have not done, to follow God's Law. Ask for his help to be truly sorry for these sins.

Prayer to the Holy Spirit

Come, Holy Spirit, fill the hearts of your faithful.
And kindle in them the fire of your love.
Send forth your Spirit and they shall be created.
And you shall renew the face of the earth.

Ask Yourself

- Have I used God's name and the name of Jesus with respect?
- Have I honored God by saying my prayers?
- Have I done my best to pay attention at Mass and to pray and sing with my parish?
- Have I shown love to my parents and others who care for me by listening to them and always doing what they ask?
- Have I lied to my parents or my teachers?
- Have I been helpful to my brothers and sisters? Have I been kind to them?
- Have I treated others in a kind and friendly way, or have I been mean to them?
- Have I played fairly?
- Did I call someone names or tell lies about them?
- Did I share with others?
- Have I treated the belongings of others carefully? Have I taken what does not belong to me?

Act of Contrition

O my God,
I am sorry and repent with all my heart
for all the wrong I have done
and for the good I have failed to do,
because by sinning I have offended you,
who are all good and worthy to be loved
    above all things.
I firmly resolve, with the help of your grace,
to do penance,
to sin no more,
and to avoid the occasions of sin.
Through the merits of the Passion
    of our Savior Jesus Christ,
Lord, have mercy.

List of Prayers and Practices

Acknowledgments

The scriptural quotation on the back cover is from the *Good News Translation®* *(Today's English Version, Second Edition)*. Copyright © 1992 by the American Bible Society. All rights reserved. Bible text from the *Good News Translation (GNT)* is not to be reproduced in copies or otherwise by any means except as permitted in writing by the American Bible Society, 1865 Broadway, New York, NY 10023 (www.americanbible.org).

The prayers from the Mass on pages 7–21, and the Apostles' Creed on page 29, are from the English translation of *The Roman Missal* © 2010, International Commission on English in the Liturgy Corporation (ICEL) (Washington, DC: United States Conference of Catholic Bishops, 2011), pages 513, 514, 515, 516–517, 522, 523–525, 527, 530, 531, 532, 640, 663, 667, 669, 673, and 528. Copyright © 2011, USCCB, Washington, D.C. All rights reserved. No part of this work may be reproduced or transmitted in any form or by any means, electronic or mechanical, including photocopying, recording, or by any information storage and retrieval system, without permission in writing from the copyright holder. Used with permission of the ICEL. Texts contained in this work derived whole or in part from liturgical texts copyrighted by the International Commission on English in the Liturgy (ICEL) have been published here with the confirmation of the Committee on Divine Worship, United States Conference of Catholic Bishops. No other texts in this work have been formally reviewed or approved by the United States Conference of Catholic Bishops.

The Act of Contrition on page 52 is from the English translation of *The Order of Penance* © 2023, International Commission on English in the Liturgy Corporation (ICEL), 45. All rights reserved. Used with permission. Texts contained in this work derived whole or in part from liturgical texts copyrighted by ICEL have been published here with the confirmation of the Committee on Divine Worship, United States Conference of Catholic Bishops. No other texts in this work have been formally reviewed or approved by the United States Conference of Catholic Bishops.

The prayer on page 51 is taken from *Catholic Household Blessings and Prayers, Revised Edition,* by the Bishops' Committee on the Liturgy (Washington, DC: United States Conference of Catholic Bishops [USCCB], 1989), page 157. Copyright © 1989 by the USCCB. All rights reserved.

All other prayers and practices contained herein have been verified against authoritative sources.

During this book's preparation, all citations, facts, figures, names, addresses, telephone numbers, internet URLs, and other pieces of information cited within were verified for accuracy. The authors and Saint Mary's Press staff have made every attempt to reference current and valid sources, but we cannot guarantee the content of any source, and we are not responsible for any changes that may have occurred since our verification. If you find an error in, or have a question or concern about, any of the information or sources listed within, please contact Saint Mary's Press.

This book was developed and designed by the expert teams at Saint Mary's Press.

Printed in the United States of America

4419 (PO7230)

ISBN 978-1-64121-247-2